FIRE BOMBERS
in ACTION

Barry D. Smith

Motorbooks International
Publishers & Wholesalers ®

First published in 1995 by Motorbooks International Publishers & Wholesalers, PO Box 2, 729 Prospect Avenue, Osceola, WI 54020 USA

Motorbooks International books are also available at discounts in bulk quantity for industrial or sales-promotional use. For details write to Special Sales Manager at the Publisher's address

Library of Congress Cataloging-in-Publication Data
Smith, Barry D.
Fire Bombers in Action/Barry D. Smith.
    p. cm. — (Motorbooks International enthusiast color series)
Includes index.
ISBN 0-7603-0043-7
1. Airtankers (Forest fire control) 2. Aeronautics in forest fire control. 3. Airtankers (Forest fire control)—California—Los Angeles Region. 4. Aeronautics in forest fire control—California—Los Angeles Region. I. Title. II. Series: Enthusiast color series.
SD421.43S58   1995
634.9"618—dc20 95-22537

On the front cover: CDF Tanker 73 dropping a water and foam mix during an operational experiment. While foam works very well with helicopters, the higher speeds when it is dropped from a tanker cause it to create too much foam which just blows away.

On the back cover: A Bell 212 on contract to the Forest Service drops a load of foam across a raging brush fire. *Photo copyright by Rocco DiFrancesco.*

On the title page: Ground crew rush to reload a military C-130 tanker belonging to the Air National Guard. They are hooking up electric power, retardant hoses, and compressed air lines to recharge the internal air tanks.

On the frontispiece: A CDF helicopter picks up a load of water from a stock pond. A water source at least four feet deep is preferred.

Printed in Hong Kong

Contents

Introduction

6

Chapter One
Life At A Tanker Base

9

Chapter Two
Air Tankers

21

Chapter Three
Helicopters

51

Chapter Four
Smokejumpers

83

Index

96

Introduction

Air tanker pilots have been asked to do some strange things, but this request was definitely one for the books. A raging fire in a Redding, California, lumber mill was threatening many structures and could wipe out the center of town if it spread. City officials asked if a tanker based at Redding could attack the fire and try to put it out.

One of the pilots said he would give it a try and climbed into his B-17 tanker. Flying over the city, he could see that the approach to make the drop left little room to maneuver. To make matters worse, there was a church on one side and several buildings closely surrounding the fire. If his drop missed, he could easily destroy the very buildings he was being asked to save. Turning onto the drop run, the pilot brought the B-17 very low to the ground, much lower than on a normal drop. At what he thought was the right moment, the pilot dropped his load, pulled up, and prayed it would hit only the fire. His drop was right on target and slowed the fire enough for the city firefighters to put it out before it burned any other buildings.

A photograph in the paper the next day showed the tanker so low that the retardant was hitting the ground while still coming out of the tank.

Not all tanker flights are as interesting as this one, but every one has its own challenges. Needless to say, pilots must be masters of their aircraft to operate them safely in the conditions found above a fire. Many of the pilots claim that flying tankers is the toughest and best flying there is in today's world of rules and regulations.

The story of aerial firefighting is as much a history of aviation as a whole as anything else. As early as the second decade of this century, people realized the benefits of using aircraft on wildland fires. As aeronautical technology has advanced, so has aerial firefighting.

Today, airplanes and helicopters perform every kind of mission imaginable. They act as the eyes of the ground commander, including seeing through smoke with special cameras; they drop retardant to form a barrier in front of the fire; they drop water and foam directly on the fire; they transport fresh crews to the lines and take out exhausted ones, and even drop crews by parachute. In the following pages I have tried to not only document the past, present, and future of aerial firefighting, but have also tried to give the reader a look at the human side of the story. I have talked for hours with pilots and crews to try to paint a true picture of their

The B-17, one of the most famous bombers of World War II, was also one of the best air tankers of the 1960s and 1970s.

jobs. Whenever possible, I flew along with them to get an idea for myself what their world is about.

The credit for any success of this book lies with the hundreds of people I came into contact with over the several years it took to put this book together. Any fault for mistakes lies with myself, for I was given ample opportunity to get it right.

Chapter One

Life at a Tanker Base

The summer sun blazes down on the quiet airport, softening the asphalt and thinning the blood. No one moves around much, it takes too much effort. A few are reading paperbacks, and a couple more watch a video. Several are napping in various locations—the porch, in front of the TV, on the lawn under the big oak. An occasional airplane strains against the heat to take off, a noisy reminder of why they are here.

The fire department radio has been pretty quiet all day; a couple of medical aids, a vehicle fire, a car accident. The magic words "vegetation fire" are now spoken, and anyone who has been asleep is instantly awake. It has been over a week since the last fire, and everyone is getting bored. A few make quick trips to the bathroom while others gather around the radio to hear more details. As the dispatcher tones out the various units, the pilots know it will be a big response. The copilots run to their aircraft to start the engines while the

captains wait to hear the exact location. Everyone is ready long before the alarm bell sounds. With a whine, several coughs, and a blast of noise, propellers become a blur of motion as engines are brought to life. The small air attack ship is the first off. It is less complicated and slower than the others. It carries the Air Attack Officer (AAO) who will direct the air tankers that will follow. As their engines warm up, the tankers quickly taxi out to the runway and apply full power. The noise starts as a deep roar and grows quickly to a high-pitched howl that assaults the ears.

As the aircraft disappear in the distance, the tanker base crew waits by the radio for word from the air attack ship on the size of the fire. The reloaders check their equipment and make plans for turning the tankers around quickly.

The air attack ship arrives at the fire and begins to orbit 1,000ft above. As the tankers arrive, they take up orbits around the fire below the air attack ship. Talking with the ground commander, the AAO develops a plan of attack and passes it to the tanker pilots. One by one, the tankers leave their orbits and make their runs at the fire, each one building on the line of

LEFT
S-2 tanker being reloaded with 800gal of retardant. The person on the right is in radio contact with the base manager and incoming air tankers.

Pilots and ground crews playing baseball between missions on a large fire. The military C-130 transports in the background are being used as air tankers.

red retardant dropped by the previous tanker. This fire is going to take several hours to contain, and the AAO tells each tanker to reload and return.

This is what the reloaders have been waiting to hear. Quickly they get into their orange coveralls and prepare the hoses. As each tanker returns, it will be directed to a certain reloading site called a pit. Each pit has its own entrance and exit to the taxiway for quick access to and from the runway without interfering with other tankers. Most bases have four pits.

As each aircraft comes to a stop at the pit, it shuts down its engines. The reloaders advance a 2.5in diameter hose and hook it into a receptacle. Every air tanker in the country has the same size receptacle so it can be reloaded anywhere. The pumps are turned on and the retardant, called mud because of its consistency, enters the tanks at 400gal per minute.

The retardant is mixed and then stored in large tanks of 15,000–25,000gal capacity, depending on the base. Most bases can

An SP-2H tanker being loaded with 2,000gal of retardant.

store from 60,000–80,000gal of mixed retardant at one time. A forklift is used to lift large bags of dry retardant above a hopper. It is dropped in, mixed with water, and then pumped into the storage tanks. Large diameter pipes run from the tanks to the pit area. The loading hoses have wheeled dollies to make moving them easier for the reloaders.

Overseeing the entire operation is the base manager. The base manager is employed by the agency that operates the base, either the US Forest Service (USFS) or the California Department of Forestry and Fire Protection (CDF). A good analogy for an air tanker base is that of a stationary aircraft carrier and the base manager is the air boss, controlling everything that happens on the flight deck. The base manager's job

NEXT PAGES
Tankers grounded by heavy smoke sit at the Stockton, California, air tanker base. As many as fifteen or more tankers may use one base on a large fire.

Aerial view of the Redding, California, air tanker base. Notice the separate taxiways to and from the reloading pits.

is to coordinate all activity on the base and make sure the tankers get in and out as quickly and efficiently as possible. On a big fire, as many as fifteen or more tankers may be using one base. The base manager monitors the fire radio to get an idea of how the fire is progressing and to allow him advance warning of when each tanker is returning. Every tanker is supposed to radio in to the base when it is a few minutes out. This gives the base manager time to plan where he will reload each tanker. Eventually, the tankers will need to refuel, and he needs to plan for that as well. If a

tanker has a mechanical problem, he has to figure out where to put it while it is being worked on. In addition, he and his staff are responsible for ordering fuel, more retardant, arranging motel rooms for out-of-area pilots spending the night, keeping track of hours flown, and all the other paperwork necessary to see that the proper agency gets the bill for the tankers.

Hemet-Ryan Air Attack Base in southern California, is considered to be the busiest tanker base in the world. It is a combined USFS and CDF base with four tankers, two air attack ships, and a heli-

ABOVE
Tanker 16, an SP-2H sits in front of the Redding air tanker base. Built in 1987, it is one of the most modern tanker bases in the country.

RIGHT
The ramp at the Hemet-Ryan tanker base in southern California. Tanker 02 is a DC-4 that carries 2,000gal of retardant.

copter. It averages pumping 1.1 million gallons of retardant every fire season. In 1980, the base pumped over 3 million gallons in six months. A record was set in September of 1985 with thirteen tankers flying sixty-one missions and dropping 70,400gal in just four and a half hours. The one day record for Hemet is 225,000gal. The location of a tanker base is determined by several factors. The most important is distance to potential response areas. This is based on historical and potential fire threats. The runways have to be of certain length to operate different types of aircraft. Some bases can handle smaller tankers but not the larger types. It is also desirable to use an airport that doesn't have a lot of traffic so the tankers can get in and out quickly.

Life at a tanker base has its own routine. The pilots come in at about 10 AM and are on duty until thirty minutes before official sunset. They go out to their aircraft and run up the engines to make sure everything works properly. If a pilot is coming in from a day off, he will taxi his aircraft back to one of the pits. When a plane is off duty, it is moved off the base so it is not in the way.

The crews wander back in and talk and read the paper for an hour or so. The usual topic is the previous night's "safety committee meeting" at the local bar and grill. Everyone then settles in for the day's wait. A week or more can go by without a single drop. Some pilots turn to hobbies to occupy the time. Some play cards or chess, others build intricate model airplanes. Reading and videotapes are also popular. At one base, two pilots worked on woodworking projects the entire season and were nicknamed the "Beaver Brothers."

Almost everyone picks up a nickname at one time or another. "Mr. Magoo" was a

A bag of dry retardant being loaded into a mixing tank. Water is injected into the tank and mixture is sent to storage tanks.

pilot who wore thick glasses. Then there were the "Two Old Fat Guys," "Shakey Jake," "Captain Bunker" (he hated everybody), "Colonel Slug," "Big Foot," and many others. Two pilots were christened the "Blunderbirds, Ace and Spinner" after they made a formation pass over the base following an air show featuring the US Air Force Thunderbird Flight Demonstration Team.

Stress levels run high when the pilots don't fly for several days, and all kinds of gimmicks have been thought up to blow off steam. A scrapbook at one base detailed some of these activities over the years. A unicycle was popular for awhile. So was riding bicycles backwards (that didn't last too long). Radio controlled model airplanes were good, as long as they weren't crashed too often (which they were). Someone even put up a basketball hoop on the wing tip of one of the tankers. They figured they might as well get some use out of the plane if it wasn't going to fly.

Boredom often leads to practical jokes. Fake body parts hanging out of an aircraft is a favorite, as are fake bullet holes on the windows. Once, some pilots put the vibrator from a dry retardant tank, used to keep the powder from clumping, on the base manager's tower. Everyone inside thought there was an earthquake and bailed out fast.

Many jokes play on the emotions of the victims. One pilot recently made captain, so the other pilots made him the target and slowly lined his cap with newspaper so it got tighter and tighter over several days. He finally figured it out but didn't say a word. Another pilot accidentally flew over President Reagan's western White House. The other pilots had someone call him, identify himself as being from the Secret Service, and order him to appear at the Federal Building in Los Angeles several days later. Another call postponed the meeting, making the pilot sweat it out even longer. The caller gave his name as Richard Tracy.

The crew of CDF helicopter 205 based in Vina, California, wash down the ship after a fire.

Copter 14 a Bell 205, of the Los Angeles County Fire Department has just finished having its water tank filled.

Other jokes are based on friendly rivalries. Some bases have both helicopters and air tankers. One helicopter pilot was sensitive about other people using his desk. While he was out on a fire, the other pilots moved it outside. When the helicopter was on its way home, he was told to land at pit 8 since that was where his desk was located.

18

Others are based on not so friendly rivalries. The military uses some of its cargo transports as tankers during extremely busy fire seasons when all tankers are committed. They are seen by some pilots as taking jobs away from their companies. One pilot threw some hydraulic fluid into the wheel well of one of the military tankers so it looked like it had a leak. It drove the ground crews crazy because they couldn't find anything wrong. It took them three days to figure out that the aircraft didn't even use the type of fluid that was found in the wheel well.

Tanker pilots don't fit a mold. There is no stereotype. They don't even fit the general stereotype of a pilot: no big watches, no leather jackets, no special type of sunglasses. Most wear jeans and tennis shoes. About the only thing that is common to all is their love of flying and their independence. The idea of an airline-type job with all its regimentation is repugnant to them. They like to make their own decisions and want very little supervision. Around outsiders they are very quiet. They don't brag about what they do. The money isn't very good, but the flying is great. There are few openings each season. One pilot jokingly said that openings occur only when someone retires or dies. The common saying among the tanker pilots is, "It's a great life if you don't weaken."

Aero Union, a large air tanker operator, uses this Piper to transport personnel around to the different bases where its aircraft operate. It is painted in the same scheme as its tankers.

Chapter Two

Air Tankers

There were many unsuccessful attempts to use aircraft to fight fire before the right combination of technologies and tactics were discovered. The first occurred in 1930 in the state of Washington with wooden beer kegs dropped from a Ford Trimotor. The idea had promise, but the aircraft of the day couldn't lift the necessary amount of water to be effective.

The next serious attempt didn't occur until after the end of World War II. Surplus Boeing B-29 Superfortress bombers and Republic P-47 Thunderbolt fighters dropped tanks which held 165gal of water. A small explosive charge detonated fifty feet above the ground to spread the water.

During the summer of 1947, the two aircraft dropped about 150 tanks on thirty test fires and five actual fires. The P-47 was more effective even though it could only carry two tanks on each flight. The tanks were not stable and tended to tumble after being dropped. Since the P-47 dropped from lower altitudes, it was more accurate. The Army Air Force recommended that one group of thirty

LEFT
CDF Tanker 93 just after it has dropped its load. The tank doors are still open.

B-29s and one group of seventy-five P-47s be deployed operationally. However, the money for such a large operation was not available and the program died.

The next step forward was one of those twists of fate that could have easily been overlooked. The Douglas Aircraft Company of Long Beach, California, was flight testing the prototype of their new four-engine DC-7 airliner in 1953. Water, held in a series of tanks that could be quickly dumped, was used as ballast to represent the weight of passengers.

During testing of the dump system, the engineers discovered the water went all the way to the ground. Douglas officials thought it might have a firefighting application and contacted the Los Angeles County Fire Department. Douglas, the Los Angeles County Fire Department, the CDF, and the USFS conducted a series of tests in December of 1953.

Events progressed rather rapidly from this point. In 1954, "Operation Firestop" was hosted in southern California by several agencies. This event investigated every possible method of suppressing wildland fires. An ex-World War II Grumman TBF Avenger torpedo bomber was fitted with a 600gal wood-

A C-130 from the 146th Tactical Air Wing of the
California Air National Guard dropping water
during a training exercise.

en tank in its bomb bay which dropped a pattern of water 90ft wide and 270ft long.

In 1956, a "squadron" of seven crop dusting biplanes were converted to air tankers and used in northern California. A small plane was used to carry a Forest Service official to direct the tankers and coordinate with the firefighters on the ground. The first month they were used on a dozen fires and were considered very effective.

Early on, the pilots discovered that much, if not all, of the water evaporated before it hit the ground on extremely hot, dry days. In 1956, a mixture of one gallon of water and 4–5lbs of sodium calcium borate was used to treat the fuel ahead of the flames. However, this mixture was found to be toxic and would sterilize the soil. Bentonite was substituted for borate.

In 1963, one of the current materials in use, diammonium phosphate, was introduced. In addition to retarding the fire, this material is a fertilizer. Several other chemicals were added to reduce corrosion, thicken the solution, and to dye it red for visibility. The main ingredient, a salt, reacts to the heat of the fire by releasing noncombustible gases which dilute the combustible gases given off by the burning fuel. The thick coating of the retardant excludes oxygen from the fuel preventing it from burning.

From 1956 through 1960, several tests were done on various types of aircraft and tank configurations by CDF and the USFS. Most were ex-military bomber aircraft. They were cheap, spare parts were available in large numbers, and the bomb bay could easily be fitted with a water tank.

The CDF was one of the first agencies to put a viable air tanker system into effect in the US. It remains the only state agency to

Tanker 130, a C-130 owned by Hawkins and Powers, and Tanker 61, a DC-7 owned by TBM, Inc. Each of these ships can carry 3,000gal of retardant.

cover its entire territory with a system of bases for aerial firefighting.

Through the late 1950s and all of the 1960s, CDF contracted with many private companies to provide air tankers. By the end of the 1960s, CDF wanted to standardize on one design. In 1969 and 1970, CDF and the Forest Service performed a study of using Grumman S-2 Trackers as a new medium tanker. The S-2 was a twin-engine, piston-powered aircraft used by the US Navy as an anti-submarine plane aboard aircraft carriers. The Navy was retiring large numbers of them in the late 1960s and early 1970s. A total of fifty-five aircraft were obtained from the Navy and eighteen converted to air tankers. Several have

The dump tubes of the MAFFS system. In the background can been seen one of the onboard retardant tanks. Each tube is 18in in diameter.

CDF Tanker 92 dropping a load in front of a spot fire. The smoke can be seen just under the drop.

Retardant drops can keep spot fires small until ground crews can reach them.

crashed and been replaced from the pool of extra aircraft. In addition to the original fifty-five aircraft, another 150 aircraft have been stripped of $30 million worth of spare parts.

The Cessna O-2, a military version of the Cessna Skymaster, was chosen by CDF for its air attack aircraft. One of these is assigned to each air tanker base and carries the AAO who directs the air tankers and coordinates the drops with the ground incident commander. Whereas CDF owns the S-2 tankers and the O-2 air attack ships, the pilots, mechanics, and all maintenance are provided by a commercial operator on a multi-year contract.

There are thirteen air attack bases located throughout the state. No base is located more than twenty minutes flying time from any CDF response area. CDF and Forest Service aviation resources work closely throughout the state, both operationally and in research and development. CDF, the

This CDF S-2 tanker has just opened two doors of its tank.

Forest Service, the Bureau of Land Management (BLM), and the US Office of Aircraft Services have a letter of agreement to attack a fire with the closest air units, regardless of jurisdiction. The responsible jurisdiction then pays the other for that assistance.

The AAO at each CDF base has many responsibilities. The first and foremost is the coordination of all aerial resources above the fire. This includes air tankers, helicopters, and smokejumper aircraft. He also acts as a set of eyes for the incident commander on the ground. The air attack ship is often the first on the scene. He can guide in the ground units, tell them if any buildings or people are endangered, the exact location of the fire, how big it is, where it is going, and request additional equipment if needed. Once other equipment arrives, he can recommend where to place hand crews, fire engines, and bulldozers. He also watches out for personnel who may not see a dangerous situation developing.

The AAO has to keep track of who is on scene, where they are, and how to sequence them into the pattern. Between tanker drops, the helicopters move in and work on the fire. They move out when the tankers make their drop runs. If smokejumpers are to be used, a break in the tanker drops has to be made. Add to this the constant updates and recommendations he gives to the incident commander and you realize that he is one busy person.

Southern California has unique problems for the AAO and tankers alike. Air traffic is so dense that the possibility of collisions is very real. Small private planes, airliners, and military jets all use certain mountain passes to enter and leave the Los Angeles Basin. If a fire is along one of these routes, the firefighting aircraft must be especially alert for other aircraft. On more than one occasion, pilots have had to maneuver violently to escape a collision.

The tankers check in when they are about five minutes out. The S-2 carries a single pilot. It is equipped with a four door tank

Tanker 64, an ex-military C-130, is owned by TBM, Inc. It is equipped with Aero Union's computer controller tank which greatly increases the tanker's versatility.

27

Tanker 00, a P-3A owned by Aero Union. This is one of the new generation of air tankers that will see service well into the next century.

that holds 800gal of retardant. The pilot can open one, two, or all four doors at once. In light grass, a trail drop with each door opening in sequence can make a long trail of retardant. In heavier fuel, trail drops can be made using two doors at a time. It is rare to open all four doors at once as it is wasteful and can be very destructive. The 800gal of retardant weighs 7,200lbs and can overturn fire trucks, uproot trees, and easily kill anyone hit by it.

The S-2 is considered a good, solid air tanker. As a plane designed to fly off and on an aircraft carrier, it has good low speed char-acteristics, is very maneuverable, and is built tough enough to take the force of carrier landings. This has come in handy when some have collided with trees and other obstructions. One S-2 collided with another aircraft and lost twenty-five percent of one wing and the entire aileron off that side and still made it home.

The S-2 is well suited for quick responses. It gets off the ground rapidly, usually within five minutes. It cruises at 180mph which gets it to a fire quickly. It is very responsive on the controls and can get into tight spots where larger tankers can't maneuver. It can carry a full load of fuel and retardant which allows it to work for three to four hours without refueling.

The major performance disadvantage to the S-2 is that it is what is known as "short coupled." It has a short body in relation to its wing. This makes it pitch up rather severely when it drops its load. Dropping all four doors at once can put it on its tail. When it stalls at low speed it gives little warning. Over the years nine of CDF's S-2s have crashed, killing ten pilots.

A tanker pilot's worst nightmare is to lose an engine on the drop run. At this point he is slow, low to the ground, and heavily loaded. He likes to plan an escape route that

This shot shows how close tankers can drop to ground units. It also demonstrates their accuracy as the edge of the burning area can be seen directly below the falling retardant.

ABOVE
The SP-2H has an internal tank and only two doors that are computer controlled to adjust the amount and rate of each drop.

LEFT
While the P-3 is disappearing into the smoke from this angle, the air below the smoke and in front of the tanker is relatively clear.

goes downhill to give him time to jettison the load and gain some airspeed. A tanker pilot never wants to drop uphill or have to climb after a drop.

The turbulence can be extreme for the tankers which drop at 100 to 150ft above the ground. Some air tankers have actually had structural damage from turbulence. There are times when there is too much turbulence and the tankers are grounded.

In addition to throwing the tanker around, turbulence can play havoc with a retardant drop. Pilots have had the retardant which was dropped by the aircraft in front of and below them lifted up by the heat of the fire and coat their aircraft bright red. Some loads are lost in the convection currents of the fire for several minutes. If and when it comes down, it is nowhere near where it was dropped.

With the S-2 and the O-2 getting old, CDF is looking for replacements for both. The main problem with the S-2 is it's aging engines, which haven't been produced in over thirty years. CDF goes through about ten to twelve per season and is quickly using up the ones in storage. The S-2s are also developing corrosion problems which will limit the life of the airframes.

No decisions have been made about a replacement. All of the possible candidates are too expensive for the department. However, even with the fiscal crisis in the early 1990s, CDF is committed to long-term upgrades to their aerial-firefighting resources.

After the disastrous fires of 1993, the Los Angeles County Fire Department leased two Canadair CL-215T twin-turboprop air tankers from the Quebec, Canada, provincial government for the 1994 fire season. These are amphibious aircraft that can land at an airport to be loaded with water or retardant.

They can also land on a lake and scoop up water to drop on the fire. They can carry 1,600gal of water and have the capability to carry foam concentrate as well.

Tankers on federal contracts tend to be of 2,000–3,000gal capacity. While each tanker is assigned to a specific base, they can end up anywhere in the country. They might be assigned to a base in California and be sent to Alaska or Minnesota. They could be gone for days or even weeks.

A lead aircraft is used by the Forest Service to guide the tankers to their drop point. The lead ship flies about one half mile ahead of each tanker and describes to the pilot by radiothe location where the tanker is to make its drop.

The tanker pilots don't seem to like this system as much as CDF's air attack style of direction. With a lead ship, the tanker pilot is giving up some of his ability to choose entrance and exit routes to the lead pilot who is flying a much smaller and more maneuverable aircraft. However, since tankers can come from anywhere in the country, the pilots will not be familiar with the local winds, weather patterns, terrain features, and other obstacles. The lead ship pilots usually stay within their own area and are very familiar with local conditions.

Flying a large tanker is different than flying the smaller, more maneuverable models. The big tankers are often ex-transports and airliners from the 1940s and 1950s. They were never meant to be flown close to the ground. It takes time to change direction so the pilot must plan his route over the fire very carefully.

The height above the ground during a drop is critical. If the drop altitude is too high, the retardant will disperse and a hot fire will burn through it. If the drop is too

CDF Tanker 76 dropping 400gal of retardant on a timber fire in the San Francisco Bay Area.

low, the retardant is wasted by covering too small an area. A low drop can also cause devastating damage to people and equipment. If a large tanker is too low, its wake can stir up the fire and send embers in all directions. A typical drop altitude is 150–200ft above the ground.

Aerial firefighting tactics are greatly influenced by the wind. The best drop is made into the wind. This causes the retardant to slow quickly and drop straight down, enabling it to penetrate through trees and brush. A drop made with a tailwind can drift and scatter. A crosswind can blow the load sideways several hundred feet. The pilots may be able to compensate by offsetting the drop point and letting the load drift onto the target.

In mountains, unpredictable up and down drafts can be encountered. The rising hot air of large fire will create its own winds. This turbulence, when added to the sudden vertical movement of a tanker as it drops its load, can cause structural failure.

Large fires can even create their own weather. Clouds of smoke can form over the fire area that reach to 30,000ft and more. One pilot described it as "flying in the door of a furnace." The smoke can form a dome over the fire. Inside this dome severe winds can be encountered that change direction frequently. A pilot might see lightning, rain, and hail in different areas of the dome.

Of course, drops that miss are not always caused by the wind. One pilot—on his first fire as a captain—pushed the wrong button and dropped his entire load on a Forest Service crew bus. No one was inside, but the windows and doors were open. For a miss, it

Air National Guard C-130 dropping a load of retardant. The 3,000gal is all dropped in one pass, which is considered a drawback to this system.

was right on target. All 600gal went on and in the bus. So much got inside it was running out the doors.

One of the most reliable large air tankers has been the Douglas DC-4, a four-engine airliner from the 1940s. Carrying a 2,000gal load of retardant it is considered to be very stable, an important characteristic for a tanker. Considering its original design purpose, it flies well at low altitudes and is fairly maneuverable. Unlike many tankers, it does not have a violent pitch up after dropping its load. It is also a strong aircraft. While other kinds of tankers have had structural failures fighting fires, the DC-4 has never recorded any major structural problems.

Most DC-4s were built for service in World War II and represent late 1930s technology. Today, more efficient and capable aircraft have become available. One of the newest tankers is the Lockheed P-3A Orion, a four-engine turboprop. The US Navy operated them as land-based antisubmarine aircraft. A newer model is still in front line service with the Navy.

The P-3A was declared to be excess property in 1989 and could be sold to civilian operators. Aero Union, of Chico, California, was the first air tanker company to convert one. Since it had never been operated by civil users, it had to be certified with the FAA who also had to approve the modifications to make it into a tanker. The interior had been packed with antisubmarine gear that had to be removed. Miles of wiring and thousands of pounds of equipment were removed. Aero Union then attached an external eight-door, 3,000gal retardant tank to the belly.

37

The Canadair CL-215, built in Canada, is the only aircraft in the world designed from the start as an air tanker. The company tried to sell some to the Los Angeles County Fire Department in the early 1980s and loaned them one for a summer. They were too expensive and did not adapt well due to the lack of water sources in the area.

The P-3 has earned high marks from its pilots. They say they finally have an airplane with enough power to really do the job. It has an excellent power-to-weight ratio which allows it to climb quickly and accelerate rapidly. These are very important characteristics for a tanker working inside canyons.

Aero Union has also developed a tank system for the Lockheed C-130 Hercules. Early models of this military four-engine turboprop cargo transport are now coming into the market and are eagerly sought after by air-tanker companies. Aero Union's conversion is rather unique. The process involves cutting through the bottom of the aircraft and installing what is essentially a bomb bay. The 3,000gal tank is above the floor of the cargo area and is removable. It has a computer controlled outlet that allows a variable flow rate to maximize the effectiveness of each drop.

The aircraft can be a tanker or a cargo plane. It can be changed from a tanker to a cargo plane in about an hour. The retardant tank can be stored anywhere in the cargo area. The plane could then be loaded with a mobile retardant mixing unit in the remaining space. This would allow the aircraft to fly to a remote airport with only a fuel source, set up a retardant mixing plant, and fight a fire. Other tankers could then use the same airport, saving time and increasing the number of drops per hour.

The military has been using C-130s to fight fires for almost twenty years. After a series

P-3 tanker beginning its drop using the burned
portion of the fire as an anchor point.

40

This is an ex-military KC-97, one of the largest aircraft ever to be used as an air tanker. It can carry 3,000gal of retardant. It is used mostly in Alaska on fires in relatively flat terrain because of its poor maneuverability. This photo was taken as it was landing at Stockton, California, during a large fire near Yosemite National Park.

Tanker 18, a DC-4, has just dropped 1,000gal of retardant in a trail drop (one door at a time) in light fuel.

of large fires in 1970, Congress asked the military to develop a retardant system that could be installed in C-130s in a short time. The system, called the Mobile Aerial Firefighting System (MAFFS), was operational by late 1973.

A series of six tanks which carry a total of 3,000gal of retardant is loaded into the cargo area of a C-130. Two 18in diameter nozzles are located on the rear cargo ramp which is left down when the system is installed. The retardant is forced out of the tanks by compressed air. The entire load is dropped in a single pass.

Four Air National Guard units each have two complete systems. Two units are located in California, one in Wyoming, and one in North Carolina. Every year, just before the start of the fire season, these units come together to train and certify crews with the systems. By law, they can only be used when all other civilian tanker assets are being used. This is to assure these military units don't take any business away from the civilian operators.

The air tanker business has come a long way in thirty-five years: from biplanes built

A P-3 dropping along the flank of a fire. While it may appear to be short, the forward speed of the falling retardant will place it right on target.

This ex-military C-119 tanker was powered by two piston and two jet engines. Its performance was marginal and it was removed from service as a tanker after several structural failures.

in the 1920s which could carry 100gal of water, to modern turboprops that can drop 3,000gal of retardant. Aircraft have gone from saving timber to saving homes and lives. As more and more people live on the edge of wildlands, the air tanker will become an even more important firefighting tool.

The PB4Y tanker is reaching the end of its useful life. It is becoming hard to maintain due to spare parts shortages.

CDF Tanker 100 has just dropped two doors or
400gal of its load.

The Canadair CL-215T is a turboprop version of the company's venerable CL-215 water scooper. The Los Angeles County Fire Department leased two for the 1994 fire season after the devastating fires of 1993.

A MAFFS C-130. The huge numbers painted on the side help the lead aircraft tell the aircraft from one another when several are working a fire. The bright orange color also helps all the other tanker pilots see them as their camouflage paint scheme makes them blend into the ground.

Chapter Three

Helicopters

As with many aerial firefighting innovations, the use of helicopters began in California. In 1957, the Los Angeles County Fire Department experimented with laying hose out of trays attached to the bottom of a piston-engined Bell Model 47. The USFS was a close partner in these tests. A short time later, they began hauling water in a bucket attached to the bottom of the helicopter by a bomb shackle. The department then tried a fixed, 105gal water tank on a Bell 47.

The Los Angeles City Fire Department began using similar helicopters as aerial observers in 1961 after a fire devastated a section of Bel Aire. It wasn't long before they also began to drop water from helicopters. By the mid-1960s, the California Division (now Department) of Forestry was also using water-dropping helicopters to fight wildland fires. Federal agencies, such as the USFS and the BLM, began contracting private helicopters for firefighting duties during this time as well.

By the late 1960s, larger turbine-powered helicopters were being used. They could carry up to 360gal of water and had room to carry firefighters who could be dropped off to attack the fire in conjunction with the helicopter.

Today, the Los Angeles City and County Fire Departments operate over a dozen helicopters. The CDF has a system of permanent firefighting helicopter stations that covers the entire state, each with an ex-military Bell Huey helicopter and crew of eight firefighters. Federal agencies operate a system of helicopters on standby and on call-when-needed contracts from private operators around the country.

These helicopters deliver water in one of two ways, either with a tank attached to the belly or by a bucket suspended by cables under the ship. Each type has its own strengths and weaknesses. The needs and circumstances of each user determine which system is used.

The Los Angeles County Fire Department developed the first tank system in conjunction with the USFS. Over the years, this tank has been redesigned and improved. It now carries 360gal of water in two sections. One or both sections can be dropped. It is used by the BLM, the Los Angeles City Fire Department, the Los Angeles County Fire Department,

LEFT
A Sikorsky S-58 dropping water through a special diffusing device that spreads out the water pattern to make it more efficient in light fuel.

many private helicopter companies and several other countries. Several private companies have also developed tank systems.

The tank is filled by a hose from a fire engine or portable pump drawing water from a stream or lake. It can be filled in under sixty seconds. The tank is best used in an arid area that has little or no sources of water. The fire departments in the Los Angeles area have identified over 100 spots where a helicopter can land to be refilled.

Pilot Lee Benson of the Los Angeles County Fire Department at the controls of Copter 16. This department hires highly experienced pilots from outside of the department, many with previous firefighting experience.

Some tank manufacturers have designed systems with a self-filling device. The helicopter hovers over a water source such as a stream, lake, or pond. A short hose from the tank is dipped into the water and is sucked into the tank by an internal pump.

The bucket system is much lighter than a tank and can be stored inside the helicopter enroute to the fire. This allows it to fly without the drag of a tank. A bucket does need a water source several feet deep, fairly close to the fire. However, since this system does not need any outside assistance from fire crews or trucks, it can be used in very remote areas. In areas with no water supplies, large tanks can be set up and filled from hydrants or fire trucks. The helicopters can then dip their buckets in these tanks.

The general rule of thumb on water drops is to start at 50ft and 50kts. Nothing is cut and dry. There are too many variables: terrain, altitude, fuel, winds. In light grass, they fly faster and lower. In heavy brush, they fly higher and slower. If they fly too slow, the rotor wash blows up more fire than they put out.

"You learn the science of dropping water from a bucket. Then you develop the art of it," according to one pilot. There is no computer or bombsight to tell the pilot when to drop and hit the fire. The pilot has to learn how to gauge the wind and his own speed. Safety may require a pilot to make a less than ideal approach. He has to learn to use wind and flight control inputs to make a good drop. For example, a fire under a tree may not be put out by dropping through the tree. By approaching from the side and banking the helicopter at the last second, the pilot can throw the water at an angle to get under the tree and hit the fire.

Lightning strikes are handled differently. Typically, there is only one tree on fire.

The best place to hit a hot, fast moving brush fire is along a ridge like this one where the fire slows down. *Photo courtesy of the Los Angeles County Fire Department.*

The ground crew can chop it down and the helicopter will hover over it at about 75–100ft. This height is used so the rotor downwash won't spread or build up the fire. If there are several small lightning started fires, the helicopter can transport ground crews to each and support each one with water drops.

The very large helicopters have their own techniques. Because of the tremendous rotor downwash from helicopters like the Sikorsky S-64 Skycrane, and the Boeing Vertol 107s and 234s, the water buckets must be slung on a cable 85–100ft below the helicopter. If not, the downwash would send burning material every-

53

LEFT
Los Angeles County Fire Department Copter 15 drops a load of water on a fire endangering the house to the right. *Photo courtesy of Los Angeles County Fire Department.*

where, spreading the fire instead of putting it out.

The pilots must make each change of direction very gentle and very smooth. With

A double door drop by Los Angeles County Fire Department Copter 15 trying to contain a late afternoon brush fire before they lose the light and have to stop flight operations. *Photo courtesy of Los Angeles County Fire Department.*

In heavy brush, a helicopter teamed with a bulldozer can be very effective in quickly containing a fire. *Photo courtesy of Los Angeles County Fire Department.*

from 8,000–25,000lbs on the end of the cable, any quick movement could start the load swinging back and forth. The pilot could find himself and his helicopter being pulled along by the load in a different direction, something he doesn't want in a narrow canyon full of fire.

A major advance in helicopter firefighting has been the introduction of foam. CDF began to experiment with it in 1987 and it is now considered standard equipment. Foam comes in the form of concentrate that looks and feels very much like liquid dishwashing soap. It is stored in a separate tank and injected into each load of water and mixed before it is dropped. The pilot can select the amount of foam based on the fuel that is burning. As the mixture is dropped, the air turbulence creates a foam.

The foam bubbles hold the water on whatever it is dropped on. It also slows down the evaporation process. This allows the water to soak into the grass, brush, or trees, greatly increasing the effectiveness of the water in preventing the vegetation from burning. It can either be dropped just in front of the fire to pretreat the fuel, or dropped directly on the burning vegetation.

Foam works particularly well on steep slopes. Plain water quickly runs down a hill without penetrating into the fuel. The foam sticks to the fuel and seeps in. Ground crews

Los Angeles County Fire Department Copter 14, a Bell 205A1. The water tank attached to the belly can carry 360gal of water and ten gallons of foam.

This helitack crew is beginning to build a line around a grass fire. They will be supported by the water drops from their helicopter.

LEFT
Gopher's eye view of CDF Copter 205 making a drop. The long, box-like canisters on each side of the helicopter are the crew steps which double as foam concentrate tanks.

can also use shovels to pick up the foam and attack the fire.

The Los Angeles County Fire Department has been investigating using foam drops on structure fires, or dropping on homes in the path of a fire as a pretreatment.

The hazards the pilots face can be extreme. Gary Lineberry, a pilot with twenty years of helicopter-firefighting experience explains: "The big fires put out a tremendous amount of heat, with a lot of updrafts, and

NEXT PAGE
A CDF helicopter arriving at a grass fire. It takes about three minutes from the time of arrival to unloaded the crew, set up the bucket, and be ready to drop water.

This CDF crew has unloaded its tools, attached the water bucket, and is sending off the helicopter to find a water source.

NEXT PAGES RIGHT
A Los Angeles City Fire Department helicopter with two firefighters rappelling to the ground in rugged terrain.

poor visibility due to smoke. You have to keep track of where all the other helicopters are to avoid collisions. There is a constant chatter on the radio. You always have a mental picture of where the others are; one at the helispot, one on the way back to the fire, one dropping in a certain location, etc. Sometimes in the fall, with the Santa Ana winds, you have to say enough is enough and shut down operations until the winds die down. It is so turbulent, you can't get down low enough to make an effective drop. I've pushed the button and the drop has been blown over the top of the helicopter. You are just wasting your time out there. A lot of risk for no gain."

The lack of visibility is one of the most dangerous hazards. Many of the firefighting helicopters that have crashed over the years have hit powerlines the pilots didn't see. Many are now equipped with special wire-cutting devices on the nose and roof of the helicopter to cut the wires before they snag the landing skids or rotor blades.

In addition to decreased visibility, the smoke can degrade the performance of jet engines. Turbines need lots of fresh air. Smoke causes sudden loss of power or even a flameout in severe cases—not a comfortable feeling when you are flying at 50mph and an altitude of 100ft with a full load of water.

On large wildland fires in the mountains, the visibility can suddenly deteriorate below safe minimums. With nowhere to go, the pilot might have to set down anywhere he can find a spot and wait for conditions to improve. This might not be until the next day. Imagine spending the night in a remote valley with fire roaring like a freight train on the ridges all around you.

While not done on a large scale, there have been agencies that have used helicopters to fight fires at night. There are some

This Bell 212 is owned by Alpine Helicopters in Canada. In extremely bad fire seasons, the Forest Service contracts with Canadian helicopter operators to fight fires once US resources are depleted.

RIGHT
A Columbia Helicopters Boeing 234 dropping its 3,000 gallon load of water on a fire in northern California. *Photo courtesy of Columbia Helicopters.*

64

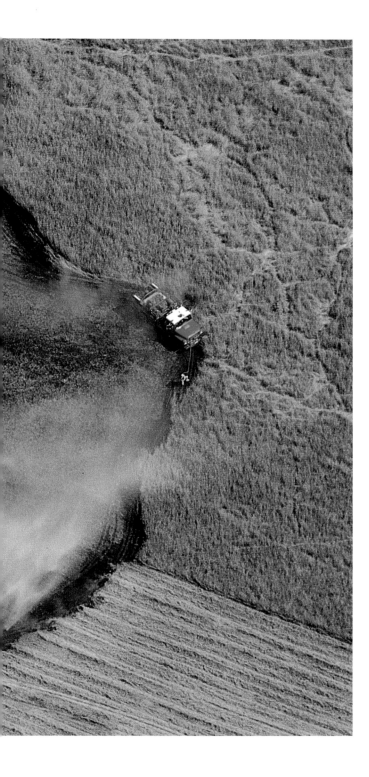

This CDF helicopter is working with two fire engines to put out this fire.

advantages. The winds usually die down at night and the temperatures are cooler. This makes the water drops much more effective so a great deal of progress can be made to control the fire.

The increase in the hazards is obvious. The Los Angeles City F.D. regularly fights fires at night. The large brush fires are not too difficult because they put out a lot of light. The difficult ones are the small fires deep in a canyon. It is very easy to get vertigo and not know which way is up or down.

The Los Angeles City Fire Department sends out a small scout helicopter with a powerful searchlight to look for powerlines and other hazards. The larger water-dropping helicopter follows and uses the light from the scout as a guide.

Other agencies have used light-intensifying devices called night-vision goggles (NVGs) that were invented to enable the military to fly night missions. For several years, the USFS had a contract helicopter in southern California with pilots trained to use these devices. The Los Angeles County F.D. also experimented with NVGs for several years until a fatal collision with another NVG-equipped helicopter occurred at a fire helicopter base. There are no current NVG firefighting helicopters in

NEXT PAGE
By varying the speed of the helicopter, the pilot can determine how thickly to apply the foam or water on the fire.

NEXT PAGES RIGHT
With fire in the foreground and a busy California highway in the background, this CDF helicopter is dipping its bucket into a canal.

ABOVE
A CDF helicopter laying down a line of foam on short grass. With this type of fuel, the helicopter can make a fast run to lengthen the drop and knock down more fire.

RIGHT
In remote areas, a CDF helitack unit might be the first on scene of a structure fire. The helicopter will drop on the structure to keep the fire from spreading into the brush.

A Los Angeles City Fire Department helicopter is using this rock to unload firefighters. You may not think so but this is in the city of Los Angeles.

California, but advances in technology could bring them back.

Firefighting helicopters are no longer used only on wildland fires. They have been used very successfully on high-rise building fires all over the world. They can rescue trapped victims and transport firefighters and equipment to the top of skyscrapers. They can also be used to hover from floor to floor to look for victims and find the exact location of the fire.

Both the Los Angeles City and County F.D.s have developed teams that are delivered and supported by helicopters to handle fires during disasters. Carrying hoses and other tools, these teams are dropped into neighborhoods that might be isolated from fire trucks by downed bridges or overpasses. They would hook directly to fire hydrants to fight fires. The same could be done in a neighborhood cut off by a brush fire or at the end of a narrow, winding road that fire trucks might not be able to drive on.

The helicopter has become one of the most useful and versatile wildland firefighting tools ever developed. More and more communities are seeing their value and purchasing them, even in these hard economic times. They can be used for saving lives and property by stopping a fire while it is still small. Who knows how many deadly fires would have swept through southern California and other areas without the use of firefighting helicopters.

The pilots and crews of the Los Angeles City Fire Department do extensive training in confined area landings and working in remote areas of the city.

Copter 1 of the Los Angeles City Fire Department loads water at one of the many prearranged landing spots in the city. Most require a fire engine for water, but a few have a ready water supply like this one.

The Bell 412 is one of the most popular firefighting helicopters in southern California. Both the Los Angeles City and County Fire Departments use them.

In addition to being used to fight brush fires, the Los Angeles City Fire Department has trained its helicopter crews to handle medical emergencies, fires in high rise buildings, and hazardous materials incidents.

RIGHT
The large amount of water and foam that can be dropped by the Boeing 107 can easily put out a spot fire that could grow to hundreds of acres.
Photo courtesy of Columbia Helicopters.

PREVIOUS PAGES LEFT
A Boeing 234 has just picked up a load of water from this small mountain lake. *Photo courtesy of Columbia Helicopters.*

PREVIOUS PAGES RIGHT
In areas with no water or only very shallow water sources, a tank can be set up for the large helicopters to dip their buckets. *Photo courtesy of Columbia Helicopters.*

LEFT
A Boeing 107 is about to dip its bucket in this river near Yosemite National Park. *Photo courtesy of Columbia Helicopters.*

RIGHT
Large fires can create an air traffic control nightmare with many helicopters dropping and dipping in the same small area. *Photo courtesy of Columbia Helicopters.*

ABOVE
Unusual viewpoint looking straight down from a Boeing 107 helicopter as it drops its load. *Photo courtesy of Columbia Helicopters.*

RIGHT
Boeing 234 dipping into a mountain lake. While extremely expensive to operate, these large helicopters are used almost every year on the large fires that break out in the far west. *Photo courtesy of Columbia Helicopters.*

Chapter Four

Smokejumpers

What I remember most about my first fire jump wasn't the jump itself. I was surprised at how independent the smokejumpers are on a fire. Most fire crews are crew oriented, with one person in charge who rarely allows independent operation of any member of a crew, let alone a rookie.

"My first fire jump was a pretty good size fire, about twenty acres. My crew consisted of ten smokejumpers. I was given an assignment to hold a piece of line and everyone else disappeared. I thought to myself, 'Well, they will be back shortly to pick me up.' I was there on my own for three hours. It wasn't like I was lost, but in my previous fire experience, you never left anyone alone like that," recalls Norm Baker, an eleven-season veteran who works out of the Redding, California, smokejumper base.

Anyone who thinks being a smokejumper is a glamorous job is in for a big surprise. It is both physically and mentally demanding. The small size of the crew requires each person to do the job of several while exercising good judgment and the ability to think and work independently.

Arriving at a fire by parachute is unlike any other type of parachuting. Baker, unlike most smokejumpers, was a sport jumper before joining the program. "In the smokejumpers, you jump on a spot you have never seen before, and never will again, in wind conditions that often vary constantly. There are no obstacles in sport jumping, just a nice big, flat, open field. Jumping fires you have trees, rocks, sloping landing zones, powerlines, and smoke. You have a limited amount of time to determine exactly where you're going to land and how to maneuver your chute. You do a lot of thinking in very little time."

Another Redding smokejumper, Tim Lum, was a paratrooper in the US Army. "On my first fire jump, the spotter pointed out the drop zone and I said, 'What opening in the trees.' I was used to drop zones two miles long and one half mile wide in the Army. This one was so small we had to drop one person at a time."

The smokejumper program was the first successful method devised to attack fires from the air. In the mid-1930s, cargo was

LEFT
A smokejumper heading for the trees. Each trainee is taught how to drape the chute over a tree to make a safe landing.

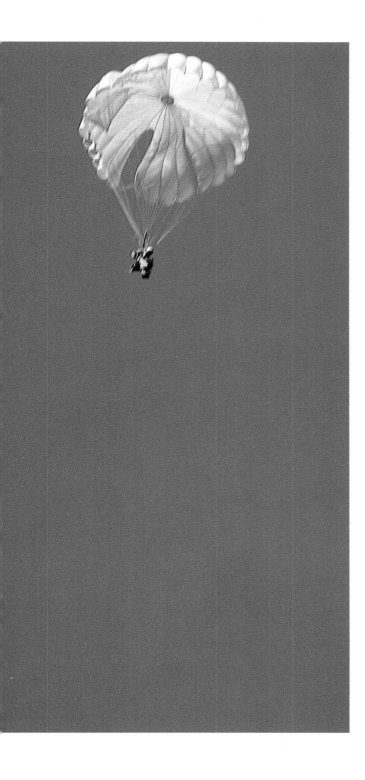

A pair of smokejumpers in the air. Each must be aware of the other's location to prevent a collision and possible chute collapse.

being dropped by parachute to firefighters in remote areas. Dropping firefighters was first tried in 1939 by the USFS in the state of Washington.

World War II almost killed the infant program. All the able-bodied men who had been involved in the expanding program went off to war. Religious conscientious objectors staffed the growing number of smokejumper bases throughout the west.

By the end of the war, smokejumpers were an accepted tool for fighting remote forest fires. They could be placed, accurately and safely, a short distance from a fire and contain it while it was small. The program has changed size and bases many times over the years. Today, a total of eleven smoke-jumper bases are operated by the USFS and the BLM in the western states.

The base at Redding, California, is typical of most smokejumper operations. The fire season usually begins in late June and can last into November, depending on weather conditions. The crews assemble in May to begin initial training for the rookies and refresher training for the veterans. The total jump crew runs about forty people from year to year. Of those, about six to eight are rookies.

The training program for the rookies is a five-week process. Each base does its own training and follows a standardized curriculum. The first week is mostly physical fitness testing. The first test consists of the candidate performing seven pull-ups, twenty-five pushups, forty-five sit-ups, and a mile and a half run in eleven minutes. There is a five minute rest between each event.

One smokejumper is out the door while another is about to exit from a C-23 Sherpa.

The rookies must pass several tests. One is the tree climbing test. They must be able to climb trees to retrieve their chutes. The objective of this test is to make sure that everyone can be taught to climb a tree without freezing a few feet above the ground. Next is the pack-out test. The students are shown how to pack their 110 pound rucksacks. They then have to walk a three mile course in ninety minutes with this load on their backs.

Each day throughout the entire training program begins with an hour of calisthenics and an obstacle course. In addition to strengthening specific muscle groups that

jumpers use, such as the ankles and shoulders, the course makes the student repeat over and over the Parachute Landing Fall (PLF). This is a technique for landing that minimizes the chance of injury. Each student performs it hundreds of times before actually making a jump.

Exiting an aircraft is practiced in full jump gear from a mockup of an aircraft cabin mounted on top of a four-story tower. Tree letdowns are practiced from the underside of this tower. PLFs are practiced from another tower which lifts the student up a cable angled at forty-five degrees to the ground and then releases them. The student

A C-23 Sherpa jump plane on a low paracargo pass. The orange and white cargo chute can be seen just opening.

can be placed in the harness so that they land going forwards, backwards, and at angles to their direction of travel. This simulates a crosswind landing.

The first training jump is done solo from 2,000ft above the ground into a large meadow. All other jumps are performed from 1,500ft, which is the operational jump height. The second and subsequent jumps are done in pairs. This is also the procedure on actual fires. The student has to get used to having a partner that he has to keep track of as well as paying attention to his own situation. This is very important, because if they

collide, their canopies can collapse, and the jumpers literally fall out of the sky.

As the jumps continue, the drop zones get smaller and smaller to make the jumps more challenging. If they don't hit the spot, they will end up in trees. Different spots are used, each one having its own wind conditions and obstacles. A minimum of seven jumps will be performed in training. During the season, each person jumps every fourteen days if they have not jumped on a fire.

When the fire season officially begins, the smokejumpers work off a master jump list to determine who goes on the next fire.

The positions on the list are chosen by lots at the beginning of the season. The smoke-jumpers at the top of the list go first and are then put at the bottom of the list. This gives each member of the crew an equal chance to jump throughout the season.

When not on fires, each person works a forty-hour work week. Much of the time is spent on training. People are cross trained in a number of areas: chute packing, mainte-nance and repair, packing cargo and equip-ment, and maintaining and repairing other equipment. Smokejumpers are also trained in loading personnel and equipment into aircraft. This is done when ground crews are shipped around the country to large fires. Smokejumpers act as loadmasters and must know how to calculate weight and balance for aircraft ranging in size from small Cessnas to Boeing 737 airliners.

When the horn goes off, the jumpers at the top of the list put their equipment on and move out to the aircraft. Each jumper wears a padded jumpsuit to help protect him from hard landings and tree branches. A motorcycle helmet with a wire mesh screen across the face protects the head. A main parachute is worn on the back, and a reserve chute is worn on the chest. Just below the reserve chute is a small backpack with food, drinking water, a sleeping bag made of paper and plastic, and other personal items for a two- or three-day stay on the fireline.

While the jumpers are getting suited up, the spotter is checking the fire's location and marking it on a set of maps. The spotter acts as the jumpmaster. It is his job to put the jumpers on the fire quickly and safely. He is an experi-enced smokejumper and works closely with the crew leader who is jumping on the fire.

Once over the fire, the spotter and the crew leader will pick the best drop zone

A student makes a parachute landing fall (PLF) in the pit of the PLF trainer.

based on the conditions. The pilot will also be consulted for his opinion. The basic guideline for drop zone selection is an area as close to the fire as possible that is safe. A downwind position is not desirable due to the possibility of the fire overrunning the jumpers. Too far away is also bad because the jumpers may have to hike a great distance to get to the fire. This may allow the fire to grow or leave the firefighters worn out before they can even start firefighting efforts.

The ideal spot is a nice flat, green mead-ow of good size. However, this is not often available. It may be a brush field or a side slope on a mountain. They try to stay away from very tall timber as this makes it difficult to retrieve the chutes after the fire is contained. An area of reseeded trees of equal height, about thirty to forty feet, is good because the canopy can be laid over the tops and the jumper will be almost touching the ground. The smallest area they would want is about 100 by 100ft. If it is this small, they would jump one person on each pass so the jumpers don't compete for the same spot.

After a tentative spot is chosen, the pilot brings the aircraft down to about 500ft above the ground to give everyone a chance to spot hazards.

Some hazards are unusual, even for smokejumpers. Baker remembers one fire that he thought would entail an easy jump. "Our drop zone was a large flat pasture with cattle grazing peacefully at one end. We had two aircraft in orbit around the drop zone and started kicking out bodies. We had four to six people in the air at any given time.

"As the first group of jumpers was coming down, the shadows from our chutes passed over the cattle, and all of a sudden they started charging across our landing zone at full gallop! We started thinking, 'Oh, no. Now where do we land?' So we changed direction and headed for where the cattle used to be before they charged off.

"Well, that spooked them again, and they went running back to their original location, right to where we moved our landing spot! This went on, back and forth, a few times until the first smokejumper landed. The cattle then ran to the four corners of the pasture, and the rest of us landed in the middle. That was the first time I ever ran into an obstacle that moved!"

This jumper hung his chute in a tree but was still able to land on his feet.

Once a spot is chosen, the pilot climbs up to 1,500ft above the ground, and a pair of weighted streamers are released directly over

89

the drop zone. They descend at the same rate as the chutes used by the jumpers and are used to measure the wind speed and direction. There is a 15mph wind limit on the smokejumpers' chutes. They may have to throw several sets due to high or changing winds.

The spotter does an evaluation of the fire and determines how many jumpers to drop on each fire. Two jumpers are usually dropped on each pass over the drop zone. Once on the ground, the crew can call for more jumpers if they need them. If anyone

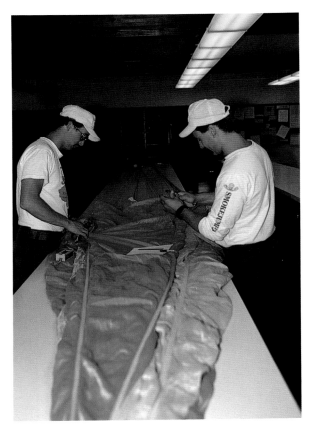

Two smokejumpers repairing a chute. Smokejumpers are taught how to maintain and repair almost every piece of their equipment.

lands in trees, they will wait until they are down on the ground before dropping the cargo packs.

A one-man pack weighs 40lbs, a two-man pack weighs 116lbs, and each chain saw weighs 75lbs. The weight of the packs may vary from base to base due to the amount of water placed in the packs. California is more arid, and therefore more water is packed. Firefighting tools include shovels, Pulaskis (an axe-like multipurpose tool), and back-pumps (a backpack containing 5gal of water coupled with a hand-pump sprayer). Crosscut saws are used in wilderness areas where power tools are prohibited.

The firefighting tactics used by the smokejumpers are basically the same as for any other wildland fire crew. They still scratch a line to take fuel away from the fire, and use natural barriers as best they can. When they build line, they may back away from the fire more because there are fewer people available and it takes longer to build a line around a fire.

A lot of fires they jump are small lightning starts. If they can get to them quickly they can attack the head of the fire while it is small and put it out. On larger fires, they may have to start at an anchor point and work up the flanks to contain it.

There is a point on some fires where the jumpers have to decide if they can handle the situation safely. "Four of us were dropped two ridges over from a small fire," Lum recalled. "The wind picked up and quickly sent it to 500 acres. All we could do was realize we weren't going to put it out, get out of its way, and simply watch it go. One thousand acres of timber isn't worth someone's life."

Once the crew is ready to leave, the crew may build a helispot for a helicopter to pick

A smokejumper has just exited a C-23 Sherpa. This is one of the Bureau of Land Management jumpers who use a free fall technique, pulling their own ripcord.

them up. If not, a helicopter might at least be able to drop a line and haul out the heavy tools. This would leave the jumpers with only their personal packs of food and water to carry out. They may have to carry everything out if a helicopter can't get to them. This averages 100 to 110lbs per person. A pack out may be only two miles or as much as ten, depending on where the nearest road is located.

The aircraft used by smokejumpers have also improved over the years. The standard jump aircraft in the 1940s and 1950s were the Ford Trimotor, originally designed in the 1920s, and the Douglas DC-3. Today, operating under contracts, the standard aircraft is a de Havilland Twin Otter twin-turboprop. The Twin Otter offers good rough-field take-off and landing qualities along with high reliability. A Twin Otter can carry six to eight fully equipped smokejumpers, depending on the air temperature (hotter air is thinner which makes the wing less efficient and produces less lift).

1991 saw the debut of a new type of aircraft for the smokejumper program. Called the C-23

Sherpa, it is a small, twin-turboprop commuter aircraft that was used by the US Air Force as a freighter aircraft in Europe. The Sherpa is a derivative of the Shorts 330-200 made by Shorts Brothers of Belfast, Northern Ireland. The Air Force used it to ferry people and small cargo among air bases in Europe, much like an overnight small package business.

The US Air Force is scaling back its operations in Europe and seven aircraft became available to other government agencies as excess property at no cost. The Forest Service took four, and the BLM took three. If bought new, each aircraft would have cost about $3 million.

Under a contract administered by the Forest Service, each aircraft underwent modification for smokejumper operations at a cost of $110,000 per aircraft. Windows, cabin insulation, and interior cabin linings were installed. A new radio system was installed along with other equipment needed for jump operations. The camouflage paint was removed and replaced with a bright white and orange paint scheme for better visibility by other aircraft. Three aircraft were put in service for the 1991 season at Forest Service bases at Redding, California; Redmond, Oregon; and Missoula, Montana. The BLM put one in service at Ft. Wainwright, Alaska. The remaining aircraft went into service in 1992.

The Sherpa has a useful load of 7,500lbs and can cruise at slightly over 200mph. It can carry a full load of twelve smokejumpers 450 miles. The Twin Otter has a useful load of 3,300lbs and cruises at 180mph. There will still be nineteen aircraft on contract for smokejumper operations, a majority of them Twin Otters. While the Twin Otter carries less, it can operate out of much smaller airports and is more maneuverable than the Sherpa.

In some places, such as California, where helicopters used for firefighting have proliferated, the use of smokejumpers has dropped off. According to Dave Noble of the Redding, CA, base, it's not that smokejumpers aren't needed anymore; it is just that some fire managers are not fully aware of their capabilities. Noble does a lot of education work in

These jumpers are practicing rappelling in case their chutes get caught in a tree. A 100ft-long tape is carried in a leg pocket of the jumpsuit.

the off season to inform the various agencies and officials about smokejumpers.

In other areas of the west that do not have the helicopter resources, the smoke-jumpers are the only game in town to get people on a remote fire quickly. They are not used solely on the small fires, either. On large fires, they can be dropped in the remotest corners of the fire from the main firefighting activity and slow its spread.

Smokejumpers are still of tremendous value on lightning fires. It is not uncommon for one thunderstorm to start many fires in one area. Two or three smokejumpers can be dropped on each one from the same aircraft and control the fires before they can join together to burn thousands of acres.

There will never be a lack of people who want to be smokejumpers. Although the pay is low and the work hard, there is a passion that develops among smokejumpers about their work. They do something that is unusual, exciting, mentally and physically challenging, and they are rewarded by stopping the destruction of wild and beautiful places. Not a bad way to make a living!

Two trainees half way down the cable from the four story exit-training tower. The students are graded on both exit and landing skills.

The landing trainer. The student is hauled up the cable by a winch and released. A student will practice landing hundreds of times during the five-week training course.

Index

Fire Bombers Index:

Aero Union, 19, 27, 28, 37, 39,

bentonite, 23
Bell Model 47, 51
Bell Huey, 51
Boeing 737, 88
Boeing Vertol, 53, 107
Boeing Vertol 234

Canadair CL-215T, 33, 47
Cessna O-2, 25
Cessna Skymaster, 25

de Havilland Twin Otter, 91
diammonium phosphate, 23
Douglas DC-3, 91

Ford Trimotor, 21, 91

Grumman TBF Avenger, 21
Grumman S-2 Tracker, 24

Hemet-Ryan Air Attack Base, 14

Lockheed P-3A Orion, 37
Lockheed C-130 Hercules, 339

Mobile Aerial Fire Fighting System (MAFFS), 43

Pulaskis, 90

Shorts 330-200, 93
Sikorsky S-64 Skycrane, 53
sodium calcium borate, 223

Republic P-47 Thunderbolt, 21